D0893643

CUMMINGS LIBRARY
THE PINE SCHOOL
HOBE SOUND, FLORIDA

SWEDEN

T H E   F O R E S T   K I N G D O M

CUMMINGS LIBRARY
THE PINE SCHOOL
HOBE SOUND, FLORIDA

WHITE STAR

Text
Valerio Griffa

Translation
A.B.A. MILAN

Contents

1 *The three crowns that surmount the Stockholm City Hall symbolize the Kingdoms of Sweden, Norway, and Scania.*

2-3 *As in the past, wood continues to be an essential element of today's architecture, which takes its cue from the Sweden that once was. The past speaks in that home/stable where tar-covered logs tell of domestic animals and farm work, while present styles are evident in those little log houses with rust-colored paint that are practically synonymous with Scandinavia.*

4-5 *Bright colors conceal the flimsiness of these houses, whether they stand on stilts or granite. Smögen is a little miracle, a harmony of forms and colors reminiscent of a fragile house of cards.*

6 *A garland of flowers is a must, as is traditional clothing. Midsummer is celebrated around the Maypole. The summer solstice is important for Nordic biological rhythms and is celebrated with new potatoes, strawberries, herring, and homemade cookies.*

7 *Dalarna is the "town of Tomte," or Santa Claus. In the Nordic battle for the home of the jolly old elf, who is a synthesis of legends from Southern Europe and Germanic countries and tales of Northern elves, Sweden calls itself Santa's "official residence." Maybe not, but looking at this landscape, who could deny it?*

© 2003, 2006 White Star S.p.A.
Via C. Sassone, 22/24
13100 Vercelli, Italy
www.whitestar.it

All rights reserved. This book, or any portion thereof, may not be reproduced in any form without written permission of the publisher. White Star Publishers® is a registered trademark property of White Star S.p.A.

ISBN 88-544-0134-X

REPRINTS:
1 2 3 4 5 6   10 09 08 07 06

Printed in Singapore
Color separation by Grafotitoli - Milan

8 top *The reticular spire of the Riddharholm church rises over Stockholm. The church holds the tombs of Sweden's royalty.*

8 center *Tepid sunlight bathes the treetops in this Lapp landscape typical of the area between Jokkmokk and Kiruna.*

8 bottom left *Cozy, pastel-colored dwellings emerge from the deep green of the Swedish woods.*

8 bottom right *The cathedral in Old Uppsala is an enchanting example of thirteenth century Nordic architecture.*

10-11 *Just stretch out on your back under a warm blanket and look up to see what terrible wonders the winter Nordic sky has in store. "Cosmic dust" brushes the earth's atmosphere and kindles in a rapidly moving cloud of different colors like a distant echo of intergalactic wars.*

12-13 *Ottar, a ninth century Norwegian chronicler, told Alfred of England, "... in the North there are domesticated stags called rhanas...." Who tamed them? The Fenni, as Tacitus called them, or the Lapps, in Scandinavian terminology, or the Sami, the name they give themselves. Whatever name we give them, they continue to be firmly identified with reindeer.*

14-15 *Slussen, or locks. Lake Mälaren and the Baltic Sea meet here, separated by the island where the capital's original heart stands. Known as Gamla Stan or the Old City, the imposing Royal Palace stands in its northeast corner.*

Introduction

"And when you read about Stockholm, Klement, remember that I told you the truth, that Stockholm has the power to draw people...." Thus wrote Selma Lagerlöf, Nobel prize winner and beloved writer, in her "Marvelous Voyage of Nils Holgersson," the story of a child who flies all across Sweden on the back of a goose, admiring its charm through the eyes of a child. Of course, this charm is not only geographical/natural, but also urban/architectural and historical/anthropological. And that is exactly this book's task, with the due proportions and adaptations. But before we start our voyage, we should approach the country through its "international" tokens, through the images, ideas, products, and people Sweden has used to "sell" itself in the great world market of "positive stereotypes." In fact, the Swedes say, "Ropa inte hei förrän du är över bron," which means "Do not shout hello till you cross the bridge". Of course we can't cross the bridge before we know where it's going, that is, before we understand Sweden's international image. From an intellectual perspective, history runs through the delicate, sad, psychoanalyzed world of Ingmar Bergman, or the social successes of social democracy, that mixture of Protestant equality and redistribution of wealth that across a half a century of economic boom has propelled the economy and society forward together, creating a legend. Or through the Nobel prize, that strange "system" that allows the Swedes to call on themselves to sit at the table like international arbiters, deciding who is the best in the world in one or another sector. It's an immense power that reinforces the image of a Sweden that is above partisanship, allied with no one in this century. The only exception is its recent membership in the European Union, which is above all an economic decision. If, on the other hand, we see it from a sensory, emotional perspective, we have the image of Swedish actors and actresses (two fine examples are Greta Garbo and Ingrid Bergman), athletes (such as Björn Borg and Ingemar Stenmark), soccer players like the great Liedholm, and cult objects like the Volvo and Saab, like Hasselblad. Equally well recognized is IKEA's dream of filling the world's homes with the Swedish idea of form and color along with the implied virtuous idea that you can do it yourself at home too, and that this is a good way to spend your free time. Another myth runs through the heads of mostly southern European males: the blonde, pale-skinned, cool-eyed, promiscuous Swedish woman. It is a stereotype, of course, whose origins can be traced to when the comparison with the "backward" customs of the south and the "freer" habits of Scandinavians ("modern," in the common parlance of the 1960's) took root through growing mass tourism.

It's a stubborn myth, as hard to eradicate as the myth of mandolins and singers in every corner that some foreigners still expect when they come to Italy. Objects, myths, and images give us an overall idea of Sweden. The best way to approach Sweden may be to return to Nils, the child who surveys it from above. The country is in fact mostly wild, a great natural spectacle that presents us with sights that once seen can never be forgotten. It is a land 930 miles long and 186 wide, one and a half times the size of Italy, with more than half of its surface covered with forests, in particular Scotch pines and red firs.

Ancient rocks were molded by alpine mountain building and then erosion, especially during glaciations two to three million years ago. In the northern and central portion of the country, the west is domiunated by the chain of mountains that form the divide with Norway, creating Scandinavia's "spine." The mountains are more rounded and lower on the Swedish side, less dramatic. We can read the difference between the Norwegian and Swedish national characters here as well. The Norwegians are sharper, while the Swedes are more mellow, just like the form of their respective mountains. And we should know that Norwegians and Swedes, sibling peoples who cooperate fully, commonly feel a mutual dislike for each other (perhaps like all neighbors), making each other the butt of their jokes. Returning to to natural geography, the mountains descend gently east toward the Baltic, into the shallow waters of the Gulf of Bothnia. Here there are great rivers, both impetuous and majestic. Farther south the lake country begins, gently rolling and fragmented into thousands of islands along the coast. This is the home of the capital, the historic region of the Vikings and the birth of the nation. Farther south, the land becomes positively flat, elongated, reaching out toward Denmark, which is its geographic continuation. This geographic summary allows us to deduce the historic one, with the central south a "Viking" land, the south "Danish" country (Scania), and the north "wild" country, ready to be colonized, Christianized, made sedentary. The realm of the reindeer and the Lapps (as others refer to them, although they call themselves the Sami) was unknown and ignored for centuries, good for nothing but fur hunters or traders who established a monopoly with the various Sami clans. So little was known about this land that old stories say that the inhabitants of the far north, the lands of Thule, lived "like wild beasts." The Sami have always been too diverse to organize into one nation. Semi-nomadic and isolated, with a different language and practicing an earth-centered religion with shamans and ritual drums, it truly became "conquered land," with inhabitants who put up no resistance. Scandinavian and Russian monarchies introduced tributes and "civilization," a Puritan language and Christianity, and divided the territory up based on geopolitical pertinence. All this in a sense uprooted the Sami from their territory, causing dispersion, flight, and a loss of identity, bringing them to the verge of extinction. Then, in recent years, a slow recovery of identity began as Sweden's greater civic and environmental awareness encountered the Sami's blossoming ethnic identity and clear political and administrative demands. This gave rise to

bilingual schools, a law that ensures them a monopoly in reindeer breeding, a recognition of rights to their lands, and cooperation with the Sami of Norway, Finland, and Russia. For the 20,000 survivors, it brings some certainty to their future. Visitors to this land can see it all around them. The reindeer have linked the Sami back to their past, their roots, while craftsmanship and tourism have pulled them out of poverty. More and more, they are beginning to wear their colorful costumes once again, with the feeling that they are in a sort of ethnic New Age, in the positive sense of the word.

If you face north in either summer or winter, you will be rewarded with extraordinary landscapes that look more like borderlands than an actual part of Europe. Far-reaching landscapes create a certain disquietude in those accustomed to the packed cities of continental Europe where every square foot counts. But more than anything else, these lands allow us to understand the soul of the Sami, their sense of being free and in harmony with the wind. The midnight sun (an oddity that seems distinctly supernatural) and the northern lights make a visit even more interesting. But while the midnight sun upsets the biological equilibrium of man in an essentially unpleasant way (the light that caresses Arctic landscapes is in fact somehow tormenting), the second phenomenon is dramatic, and fearsome. A tempest of electrically charged particles, drawn by the earth's magnetic field, "rubs" against the atmosphere, lighting it up, like a dark presage of catastrophe, like a message from the cold stars. Even in these times of daily special effects, extraordinary games, and virtual tricks, one cannot help but be impressed by this magnificent spectacle. This land has become a world of outdoor activities, safe adventure, offering the marriage of peace and an adrenaline rush that people seek, an antidote to the harsh rhythm of the city. Here, we can peacefully paddle a canoe on the lakes or go rafting down fast, foamy rapids, in a setting so pristine that it almost seems unreal, as accustomed as we are to little pieces of nature under assault by developers. Here, we can gather mushrooms and berries in late summer in a healing return to our roots as hunters and gatherers that reawakens the senses. We can ride horseback endlessly, fish for salmon and other tasty prey, go hunting, mountain-biking, and enjoy the smell of an open fire, that special, unique flavor of grilled meat and a pot of coffee enjoyed in the out-of-doors. It is even better in winter. In December and January there is little light, when a blue duskiness envelops the world, we can meet the challenge of the cold and dark by seeking out the open air and its stimulating benefits. In March and April, the days are longer than in the south and we can stay outdoors later. What could be better than setting out at five or six in the evening, or even later, to walk through the woods, climb a mountain, or hike around a lake? Dog sleds, horses, reindeer, cross-country skiing and hiking, downhill skiing (for example, at Tärnaby, Stenmark's hometown, with a small museum that recounts his victories), heliskiing in the mountains of the "five Sami valleys" (the Norra Storfjället, ten peaks and eleven slopes, nothing but snow), trout and salmon ice fishing are all awaiting the adventure-seeker. And there's always that campfire, perhaps inside a Sami traveling tent, the *lavvu*, with a smokehole at the top and a big pot of stewed reindeer inside. It is a way to be friends with nature even when the mercury drops.

16 top Jokkmokk, on the Arctic Circle, is a Sami village. Here one of its inhabitants during the winter time.

16 bottom Vänern and Vättern are the country's two largest lakes, but all of Sweden has lakes for rowing and paddling during the long summer evenings.

17 top The Abisko National Park was established in 1909. It is an "Arctic garden" with "rounded" mountains and a large lake. Lapland's scenery is at its best in the canyon carved by the Abiskoyokka River.

17 bottom Evergreens and marshes, clearings where grass and water merge: the Swedish landscape includes corners of pristine nature like this, which can be explored on foot or by canoe.

18-19 A thin film of blue veils the atmosphere of the winter capital. Air and water, rock and bronze take on twilight hues even during the day. Even the iron spire of the Riddarholmen bell tower looks like nothing more than a vertical streak.

20-21 The T-Centralen station, or "contemporary art explained to the people." The Stockholm subway is underground art, but only because the artwork is in the underground stations, thus freed of annoying subway graffiti.

Certain cities have sprung up on the water as water is their reason for existing. It is not simply or only a question of defense or trade, but also a matter of aesthetics and philosophy. It has something to do with the architectural line that only water can create, that deep, discreet pleasure that arises from living in contact with water. Stockholm is one of these cities. It is so "aquatic" that the subject comes up constantly. One is its recent Water Prize, which does a good job of making up for what Alfred Nobel could not have predicted, by rewarding people who contribute to cleaning up the most abundant element in nature. The world's best in the sector are selected and rewarded, thus expanding awareness of the problem and the knowledge that attempts to resolve it are possible. But it does not stop here. Work is coordinated and international studies and meetings are organized in the belief that only a global approach to the problem can lead the way to the solution. The Water Prize is thus an amplifier, a sort of discreet but firm "call to order" for the entire world. Thus, yet again, it puts Sweden in a rather enjoyable first place position. Awarded each year by the royal family of Sweden in the Nobel Hall, the prize has the flavor of good conscience as well as the tangible weight of 150,000 US dollars. It is a way to recall the nature of Stockholm and its intimate link with water.

There is also the well-known, highly popular Vasa Museum, which recounts an incredible story. A royal sailing vessel was built in 1628 only to sink just a few minutes after launching. It had been a magnificent work, a gigantic effort to celebrate Swedish maritime power of the period, with a hull that was a work of art and masts over 164 feet high. The causes of its untimely demise were probably mistakes in measurements and the ship's overly large size, yet the construction remains grand, resembling something like a cathedral. At that time, Sweden was a global power, with an empire that included Finland, Karelia, the Baltic countries, Pomerania, and Bremen, and a great desire for expansion, which soon foundered on insufficient economic and human resources. However, that history, that period of stardom, has stayed with the Swedish culture, a sort of military pride in a country where the army's primary purpose seems to be providing men for UN forces. It is celebrated in the museum, along with the idea that Stockholm was once queen of the sea. Gamla stan is the old city, the original center with its seventeenth and eighteenth century palaces, the vast, unusual Royal Palace, the tall, narrow Baltic houses, and the lattice-work Riddarholmen bell tower. It is permeated with the air of bygone days, and the link with water is clear from its natural confines (the old city stands on an island) and the many nautical antique shops.

Across from Stockholm, before reaching the open sea, there are roughly 24,000 islands in a spiderweb of passages, channels, and arms of the sea that make it a universe in itself. For example take the boat to Nybrokaien, sailing on the old Waxholm III, a small, pleasant, turn-of-the-century ship that offers a cruise of

the archipelago, with stops at various islands and meals served on board. It leaves in the morning and traverses the landscapes that inspired the playwright August Strindberg and the painters of the second half of the nineteenth century, for example at Kymmendö. It also makes a stop at Sandhamn, with its fishing village, and at Vaxholm and its sixteenth century fortress. It returns in the evening to a Stockholm that by now is cloaked in gold, a radiant light that dissolves its hard surfaces in the softness of air and water. The world of the archipelago is a little like the world painted by Carl Larsson, with its fine sentiments and little things, always full of innocent optimism.

The museum house of Carl Milles is in Lidingö, just outside the city. Milles was a contemporary sculptor who filled Swedish cities with classical fountains featuring mythological characters, their elongated bodies splashing in the water. The museum is a Mediterranean villa with stepped terraces overlooking the sea, full of reminders of Roman art, trees, and flowers. Here, the works of the sculptor retrace Milles' path in his constant search for the secret of classicism. Bronze bodies demonstrate that water is the origin of man, his "vital juice," the only path of communication and interaction between the center and the periphery, and its link with the earth. It is pleasant to spend the day here, to reflect on the essence of art and water, perhaps seated in the café on the rose terrace overlooking the capital's archipelago. However the city, the most beautiful and lively capital in Scandinavia, is where the Swedish spirit can truly be sensed. For example, we can see it in the subway system, which here is not reduced to the usual mass of irritating scrawls like some sort of hymn to human lack of communication, but on the contrary is cared for like an art gallery. Each station has its forms and colors, its works of art, which become part of the people's everyday lives, to some extent shaping them. This is the concept of civilization too. Underground art has its sanctuaries at the stations of Vreten, Duvbo, Tensta, Hjuslsta, and Akalla, just to name a few. After all, it is no secret that the Swedes coexist with design. Just look at the furniture, the interior decoration, the windows, the many objects that we see right before our eyes. Stockholm is also a city of design in a global sense. This begins with architecture and urban planning, which are unique here, for example in how they treat the suburbs, seeking to make them liveable in primarily aesthetic terms. And abandoned urban areas are restored according to the concept that a modern metropolis is the algebraic sum of smaller, self-sufficient communities. Essentially, the idea is that small is good, as it provides security (i.e. better services), but so is big, as it creates dynamism and verve. This continues in applied design and food, which means New Swedish cuisine. Here in Stockholm, the concept of design pieces reaches its height, with design studios, shops, showrooms, and supermarkets. Restaurants are right behind, not just because of the interior design they offer, but because of a concept of food that is linked to research, aesthetics, and flavors, combined with the highest quality Nordic ingredients.

22 *December thirteenth (which has fewer hours of light than any other day of the year) is celebrated in every family, community, and work group, and even includes a national beauty contest in Stockholm. The focus is on Saint Lucy (a saint from Syracuse), who is played by a girl dressed in white, her head adorned by a crown of lighted candles, accompanied by other girls and boys acting as pages. They march in a procession singing a translated version of the Italian song "Santa Lucia," drink hot mulled wine, and eat cinnamon cookies.*

23 top *In the winter, some of the capital's gardens and squares become skating rinks. Schoolchildren, young sweethearts, and fathers and mothers using their children as an excuse all come out here.*

23 bottom *Skansen is a place of tradition, a museum devoted to old Sweden located in an especially beautiful part of the capital. Gatherings are often held here among the old reconstructed ninteenth century houses. Advent is a time of heightened nostalgia for the past and the little things in life. People sing, their faith renewed.*

There is a small area, perhaps a couple of square miles, where various aspects of the capital coexist and are waiting to be explored. Sergel Square (near the site of the assassination of premier Olof Palme, an unexplainable and unexpected crime of the 1980's) is above all the heart and showcase of this social democratic country, with its great rational but ugly buildings evoking the "progress" of the 1960's. From it lead large, cosmopolitan business streets worthy of an international capital. Then there is the tree-lined Kungsträdgården Square, the reign of skateboarders, people relaxing on park benches, immigrants from all over the world, young couples, night owls, and disco fans who come out in the evening and night. Farther on is Skeppsbron, with the locks that separate the Baltic Sea from Lake Mälaren. Here, as in any respectable water city, we can travel by ferry, a mode of transport that creates a stronger, livelier link with water from the olfactory perspective as well. Finally, there's Skansen, an open air museum on the island of Djurgården. Its collections commemorate the Sweden that once was, the Sweden of farmers, the eighteenth to nineteenth century sense of homeland. It's so real that it seems false, in an era dominated by the Disneyesque idea of a "park." Yet here the goal is to remember, to keep alive that part of us that seeks its roots, the little things, identity and simplicity, the customs and rhythms of a slower world, as the other part of us reaches out toward globalization of markets and identities. For example, this is the home of a ritual that arose almost as a joke in the 1920's, the proclamation of Saint Lucia of Sweden Day (December thirteenth). It is a combination of an ancient winter solstice festival, exoticism (through the translated version of the Italian song "Santa Lucia da Siracusa," creating a connection with Italy, the land of light, and the saint), and the modern commercial-voyeuristic competition for "Miss" whatever. But the Swedes benevolently pretend to believe in it, and they all dress up their own little versions of Saint Lucia. So during that week of Advent, at home, at work, and on the streets, groups of young girls dressed in white appear with crowns of lighted candles on their heads, accompanied by boys wearing conical caps and carrying wands ending in a star. They reach the dark halls, singing Santa Lucia (pronounced "lüsia"), and pass out ginger cookies and *glogg*, hot mulled wine. It is an effortlessly moving moment that usually vanishes rapidly with the *smörgåsbord* feast that follows in an endless sequence of rich tributes to the cold and winter: salmon, herring, shrimp, reindeer, salad, paté, vegetables, cheese, fruit, and dessert.

Poles apart from Saint Lucia is the Midsummer Festival (June twenty-fourth or the nearest weekend). This is a celebration of light too, but rather the light of the longest day of the year. People gather in groups (families or neighbors) around a flower-bedecked tree trunk planted in the ground in traditional costumes, with women wearing garlands in their hair. They dance around the tree and then feast on herring, new potatoes, strawberries and home-made sweets. Young people who are old enough celebrate in a more prosaic fashion: by getting good and drunk.

Drinking heavily on Friday or Saturday night is a common activity of young Swedes, especially males, and is in fact a common custom among all young Scandinavians. It is a sort of mandatory, liberating ritual in a country rife with rules where one cannot always fully express oneself (due to modesty or good breeding). As a result, beer wins out in the struggle between self-censure and rebellion, although usually only on weekend evenings.

There is also a simple, pleasant way to get to know Sweden in small doses, in a sort of enjoyable illustrated synopsis of the country. Get on an old late nineteenth century ship in Stockholm and leave the city's Baltic profile behind you (with the City Hall tower and its three crowns of the unified reigns of Denmark, Norway, and Sweden since the 1397 Kalmar Union). Slip onto Lake Mälaren and head toward Drottingholm Castle, known in these parts as the Swedish Versailles, and then head out to the sea at the Södertalje locks. This is where the route known as Göta Kanal begins, a nineteenth century work designed to link the lakes in the south central part of the country. We come to the great lakes, the Vättern and the Vänern, then sail out at Göta älv and finally Göteborg. The trip follows the slow rhythms of the water, with no possible escape or shortcut, forcing us to think, observe, and reflect for three days that teach us much more than any long, frenetic vacation could. It is a trip back into time, among medieval and Renaissance castles, Viking sites, Catholic churches transformed by the Reformation, sawmills, water mills, locks and bridges of pre-industrial Sweden, peasant cottages of rust red wood, and yellow fields of rape, a kind of turnip. The towns show the Swedish way of dwelling and coexisting together. We are led on to Göteborg, whose spirit is noticeably different from the capital's. Located in the center of the triangle whose points are the three Scandinavian capitals, the city has always opened the way to Sweden, or perhaps acted as the Swedish window to the North Sea world. The Vikings knew it when they left from here for their western trading, and the million Swedes who left for America from here between 1840 and 1940 knew it as they made their way to the hope of New York. It was a tributary of the great European river that during those years created the "third Europe" (Braudel's fine definition) between the Atlantic and the Pacific. Göteborg is both a gate and window, headquarters of the East India Company (synonymous with merchants and wealth), and the home of prestigious names like Volvo and SKF, a part of the vast web of European industrial cities. It is the mechanical industry's international headquarters, with everything good and bad that the manufacturing industry brings. This city, which the capital overshadows a bit in international affairs, wants to be number one, a competitor. It shows its desire through technological excellence, athletic challenges (Göteborg soccer is the only European level Swedish team), a monumental downtown area (see Götaplatsen with its Milles Neptune), and a wealth of art (see the Konstmuseet with its collections of paintings by Carl Larsson and Anders Zorn, nineteenth century interpreters of "Swedishness").

24 top *Like this field on the island of Gotland, in June all of south central Sweden is tinged with the hues of yellow rape.*

24 bottom *The Wilhelm Tham, a 1912 steamboat, connects Stockholm to Göteborg across the Göta Kanal.*

24-25 *Drottningholm Castle with its French-Italian Renaissance exterior and rococo and Gustavian interior, was built for Queen Hedwig Leonora in the second half of the seventeenth century.*

26 *The Malmö municipal building was built in typical Dutch Renaissance style.*

26-27 *Visby is a city of roses and ruins: roses are cultivated everywhere, and the ruins are the churches and abbeys that were destroyed during the Reformation.*

Scania, which did not become Swedish until the seventeenth century, is yet another Sweden. It is more continental, more Danish, so much so that the Renaissance city hall of Malmö has two portrait galleries, one for the Danish monarchy and one for the Swedish one. It is a land of castles, little ports, and towns built to order in the middle of large cultivated fields, forced there by their rural-urban conception. Still, Malmö is dynamic, with a great desire to find its role, which it has discovered by once again looking over toward Denmark. The siren song that calls from the Strait of Öresund, only eleven miles wide (including the island in the center), is powerful. Future scenarios will be played out here, on this arm of the sea, with the opening of the great bridge that connects Malmö with Copenhagen, and thus Sweden with Denmark. The new conurbation will probably change Scandinavian geopolitics, as half of the goods to and from continental Europe pass through

here. In essence, modern technology has united what seventeenth century wars of conquest had divided.

Gotland ("good land") is the calcareous island southeast of the capital. The Vikings used it as a base for their fur trade with Russia and the Baltic countries and also scattered the country with strange stone tombs arranged in the form of ships. In the High Middle Ages, it was a Baltic maritime power, only to be supplanted by the Hansa League. Visby, its capital, is still surrounded by walls, with the ruins of churches destroyed by the Reformation and millions of roses, a tribute to the romanticism "of flowers and rocks," which here appears most justified. In the city and on the island in general, which are elite vacation spots, we can find two interesting aspects of the Swedish world. At Visby, an open area is used by vacationing politicians to explain domestic and foreign policies (as a preview to vacationers), becoming a sort of holiday rally or Augustus-style speaker's corner. Farther north is the islet of Färo, once the *buen retiro* of Ingmar Bergman, as well as the setting for some of his first films. The island itself is unique in a Baltic fashion. A sort of rocky spur, it has long white beaches, cliffs, and an excellent bike path.

Småland is a unique region, the land of glassmakers. Glassmaking is an initiative born of court necessities. The Vasa wanted national glasses, containers, and cups, so they imported glassmakers, first Venetians and then Bohemians. By the mid-eighteenth century, it became clear that glassmaking could become an industry. This region exports glass even today, once again joining design to industry in one of the leitmotifs of Swedish success. Names like Kosta Boda and Orrefors have traveled the world, renewing a sector that elsewhere has become somewhat aged and slack.

Uppsala is the city of history, the Swedish window to the eighteenth century. An ancient capital, it is home to a bishopric and a university. It was an international scientific center in its time and a place of culture. It was home to Olof Rudbeck, who discovered the lymphatic system, Anders Celsius, who invented the centigrade scale of measurement that bears his name, and Wilhelm Scheele, one of the founders of organic chemistry. Above all, it was home to Carolus Linnaeus, the founder of modern botany, the inventor of binomial nomenclature for classifying living species, and the orderer of natural things. A person of great cultural depth, through his Systema Naturae he found the key to interpreting "creation," as it was once called. We need no reminder that his architecture of nature survived modern concepts of science just like the ideas of Galileo and Euclid. When traveling to his city, it is interesting to visit his Botanical Garden, a prototype of those later built everywhere, and a good spotlight on the eighteenth-century mindset. We can also see the seventeenth-century Theatrum Anatomicum, one of the three left in the world, where the physicians trained by analyzing cadavers.

The Sweden that has entered the European Union is a society undergoing a profound change. Ever since the 1930's, when Albin Hansson began to theorize and construct what he called *folkehammet*, i.e. "a house for people," a society of well-being for everyone, much has changed. The original and inimitable "Swedish model" adapted to change as much as it could. The economy changed completely, and the very society that grew within that model has changed totally. Unlike the Norwegians, who can afford to stay out of the European Union because they have oil to sell, Swedish industries need a large market if they are to stay afloat. Partly because of product prices, this market can only be Europe. Even Swedish society is looking more toward international customs, conduct, and consumption, to planetary ways and myths. But there is still one thing that almost everyone agrees on: nature and the environment are very important here and are considered a national genetic heritage. Those forests where we may see an elk, those lakes that are covered with first ice and then snow in winter, those rivers, peaceful or wild as a young bull, that sea with its long white beaches are in the heart of every subject of Karl Gustav. Similarly, the king, Queen Silvia, and the Crown Princess Victoria are another national "heritage," accepted and beloved as guarantors of institutions, as supporters of environmental and social initiatives, and as an institution that pays its taxes in a country that has long made taxes its credo. There is a reason why the royal motto states, "For Sweden, in step with the times." It says it all. A nineteenth century Swedish writer once said that the north is heroic and philosophical. He was right.

28 top *"Watch for Deer" signs are common on Swedish roads, and for good reason: many traffic accidents involve deer.*

28 bottom *Orrefors and Kosta Boda have been historic glass-making names in Småland since the eigteenth century. "Imported" Venetian masters first brought the art here, and the region gradually became a glass-making district, with dozens of companies still in operation even today.*

28-29 *Sövdeborg is one of the numerous seventeenth to nineteenth century castles in Scania that were built in Danish style.*

30-31 *Between January and April, many of Stockholm's canals and lakes are frozen, and some years even the archipelago freezes. The result: 10,000 members in the hundred-year-old Skating Society, come out in groups on Sunday morning to totter around on their blades, aided by a pole.*

32-33 *Dalarna is one of the regions where traditions are still alive and well. In Leksand, people still go to church in horse-drawn sleighs during the winter; during the summer they go by boat. If it is the Midsummer Festival, you will see violins among the paddles.*

Sweden in Pictures

34 top *The landscape of Jämtland in north central Sweden is distinguished by miles and miles of low hills covered with pine trees, and thousands of lakes of every size.*

34 bottom *This photo shows a view of Stockholm's archipelago. Around the capital there are about 25,000 islands and islets, a true maze of passageways to the open sea. Sailing is peaceful here, and many can afford a small house, pier, and boat.*

35 *Vättern is the fifth largest lake in Europe. The landscape is flat and undulating, with small hills that slope down to the shores of the lake and croplands that run down to the water.*

36 top *A landscape in central Sweden. A small lake, a birch tree in the foreground, a country cottage in the background, and the soft light of dusk enveloping it all. It is an idyllic picture that visitors will see often.*

36 center *Lakes and evergreens are what distinguish central Sweden. Green and blue alternate, defining the typical Swedish landscape.*

36 bottom *The waterfalls of the Indalsälven River in central Sweden are not particularly high. Still, they exude the fascination of powerful, impetuous rivers, with a force that seeks to burst out and carry everything away with it.*

36-37 *Silence still reigns in south central Sweden. A field of crops looks like green waves leading to a blue lake, with a rust-colored cottage embellished by white-framed windows.*

Lakes and Canals
in South Central Sweden

38 *A few bladder-campions nestle among the rocks. Carols Linnaeus, a professor at Uppsala, published his Systema Naturae in 1738, in which he classified and ordered nature. He invented a binomial classification that gave plants and animals a first and last name, with special emphasis on flora. He also invented the concept of a botanical garden, where plants are arranged by family and evolution.*

38-39 *The magnificent landscape of Vänern is an irresistible invitation to spend summer on the lake sailing, swimming, rowing, sunbathing, and preparing grilled meat, all activities that the Swedes traditionally love.*

40-41 *The Göta Kanal is also open to private boats. Along the way, there are hotels and numerous museums, shops, and towns to visit.*

41 top *On Lake Siljan in Dalarna, an old barge offers a lovely excursion. Traditional boats, used mostly on Sundays, and the numerous rowing races, are also spectacular.*

41 center *Lake Vänern was used as a connecting element in the great nineteenth century plan for the Göta Kanal. It is the third largest lake in Europe but is rather shallow. It offers lovely views that include reeds, smooth rocks, and numerous animal species.*

41 bottom *The Göta Kanal, completed in 1832, is 118 miles long and 85 feet wide, with 58 locks and a 299 foot drop. It took 58,000 men and 22 years to build it, just a few years before the train and dynamite were invented.*

Water
and its Forms

42-43 *Granite mamelons, the sea, canals, lakes, and marshes: Bohuslän is a land of beautiful scenery. It is undoubtealy one of the loveliest regions in the country.*

43 top *Sailing along the coast of Bohuslän is a special experience, not only because of the enchanting beauty of the landscape, but also due to the many attractions that the area offers. This photo shows Gullholmen, a small island that can also be reached by ferry.*

43 bottom *Hallevikstrand in Bohuslän is a typical little harbor: rust-colored houses, wharves, and little sailboats create an unforgettable picture.*

44-45 *Elves or Vikings? The surreal atmosphere of the Nordic forest, brimming with water and strange light, calls to mind the northern sagas, endless stories of heroes, or the magic of elves that nature herself inspires.*

46-47 *In this view of Lapland, the streaked sky, the colors of the water, the woods, and the snow are reminiscent of the gaudy hues of the traditional tunics worn by the Sami who live in this region.*

48-49 *A typical Lapland landscape is immortalized in this image: a small river is frozen into stillness by the harsh winter cold, while deep snow on its banks and snow-laden pines and firs sparkle in the early morning light before a glittering white background.*

49 *Dalarna Selma Lagerlöf, an indigenous writer who in 1909 received the Nobel Prize for literature, set many of her tales in the world of traditions and farmers. This is where her house and grave are located.*

The Colors
of the
Country

50 top *Scania is primarily an undulating plain not unlike neighboring Denmark, from which it is separated only by the Strait of Öresund. The gently rolling hills are accompanied by the sinuous movement of grain waving in the wind.*

50 center *An unpaved road runs through the dense woods of Dalarna. Here it is not rare to see horse-drawn carriages, which allow visitors to tour the area slowly, savoring the moods of the woods, at a pace from bygone times that invites us to reflect.*

50 bottom *Wood is one of Sweden's primary resources and helped support the country's industrialization. Even today, large quantities of paper and cellulose are exported while the furniture industry is rapidly expanding.*

50-51 *A country idyll among white daisies and gray summer storm clouds. This picture sets off the beauty of the Swedish summer, brief and precarious, but always lovely.*

Fairy tale reflections

52-53 *Kungälv was a frontier land during the complicated history of Scandinavia, when Denmark, Norway, and Sweden alternately dominated each other. This is the Bohus Fästning fortress, built in the fourteenth century by a Norwegian king to defend his southern lands, which did not fall under Swedish rule until the seventeenth century.*

53 *Örebro Castle, which assumed its present appearance during the sixteenth century, stands on an island in the middle of the Svartån River. Here, in 1810, the French Marshall Bernadotte was elected the successor to the Swedish throne.*

54-55 *The timeless landscape of Östergotland, in south central Sweden.*

56 top *The Tiveden National Park in the Vänern region is an extensive forest on morenic land. The park, established in 1983, is 3,336 acres in size and offers the typical flora of the borderlands between northern and southern Sweden. There are dwarf birches and holm oaks, but above all remnants of prehistoric forests.*

56 bottom *The Höga coast is in Ångermanland, part of the passage to the Great North, towards the rivers and mountains of Lapland. It takes its name from the river that traverses it, flowing from the lakes of the highlands to run impetuously into the Gulf of Bothnia.*

56-57 *Ångermanland: the beauty of this view comes from the light created by the group of birches with their tender green leaves and the red/blue houses. Sweden often offers us these patterns of color that seem painted on canvas.*

58-59 *On Lake Siljan in Dalarna, an evocative color composition honors the northern lights.*

60 *On the island of Gotland, the largest in the Baltic Sea at 74 miles long, unexpected calcareous cliffs and beaches with crystalline waters warm enough for swimming are reminiscent of famous Mediterranean landscapes.*

61 *This natural landscape is captivating in its simplicity and serenity. Despite the short summer season, on the island of Gotland the climate is mild year round, making it one of the most popular places in the country.*

Rocks and Charm

62 top left *Öland, the fortified area at Eketorp, is a prehistoric site that was inhabited until the Middle Ages and reconstructed by archaeologists. The island is a granite block 87 miles long and 10 miles wide, with a harsh terrain dotted by numerous windmills.*

62 bottom left *The windmills of Tofta in Gotland are somewhat reminiscent of those in La Mancha. Gotland, which means "good land," is a flat island swept by the Baltic wind.*

62 right *In Gotland, many Catholic churches were left to fall into ruins, and now only their outer walls are left standing. This photo shows one of the Gothic churches that the Protestants adapted to the new religion.*

62-63 *Gotland is a medieval Viking island. Baltic traffic passed through here because of the fur and amber trade with Russia, with goods traveling down the great rivers to the Black Sea, Caspian Sea, and Byzantium.*

64-65 *The county of Vastergotland offers scenery of rare beauty. The mists during the cold season girdle the forests in a close embrace.*

Nordic Architecture

66 top *The Royal Palace of Stockholm, an eighteenth century masterpiece completed under the careful hand of the architect Nicodemus Tessin, has an Italian-style façade and French interior, with 608 rooms and chambers decorated by the leading artists and craftsmen of the time. It was opened as a royal residence in 1754.*

66 bottom *The Stortorget Christmas market in Gamla Stan, the Old City, and the Christmas tree are not native traditions, but have been imported from Germany. Despite this, they are beloved by Swedes because they coincide with Advent, which in turn includes the Nordic Festival of Light on December thirteenth, now translated into the celebration of Saint Lucy.*

67 *Gamla Stan, a perfect reproduction of a medieval town, is the oldest part of Stockholm. The nucleus of the trade city was established here in 1250, long before it became the capital. Moored at the docks are the ships that will depart for the long trip to Göteborg along the Göta Kanal.*

68 *The Gold Hall in Stockholm City Hall, built in Nordic Gothic style in 1923, has walls richly decorated by Byzantine-style mosaics, the work of Einar Forseth, who used 20 million mosaic pieces.*

69 top *The Stockholm City Hall in Kungsholmen is a red brick building designed by Ragnar Östberg, the most representative architect of the Swedish romantic movement. The bell tower, 348 feet tall, has a carillon that plays twice a day and a gilt weather vane with the three crowns that symbolize Sweden.*

69 bottom *This view of the modern part of Stockholm shows the different styles that characterize the architecture of the capital and the extensive road work done in the 1950's and 1960's. Stockholm, a city of islands, is also the only one with an urban national park, a group of natural areas completely or partially adapted to human needs.*

70-71 *The Victoria Hall is one of the enchanting areas visitors can admire in the Royal Palace of Stockholm, a building that also holds the Charles XI Gallery, an admirable example of Swedish baroque, the Bernadotte apartments with the portraits of the dynasty, the Royal Chapel, and numerous museums, including the Gustav III Antiquities Museum.*

72 top left *The Norre Auktionen Palace holds an auction house that is not only the largest in the country, but the oldest in the world. Its countless items on display often include priceless objects.*

72 bottom left *The Sturecompagniet of Stockholm is an old palace with a covered inner courtyard that has become a gathering place and center for nightlife.*

72-73 Sergel Square, the capital's modern center, was designed in the late 1950's and has a lighted glass obelisk in the center. The House of Culture stands here, as well as the city's theater and other gathering places. Modern pedestrian areas for shopping are also located here.

73 The NK Gallery (Nordiska Kompaniet), is one of the department stores that offer the best of Scandinavian products, making it an ideal place for shopping enthusiasts.

74-75 *The Vasa Museum is a memorial to a resounding failure: the sinking of the Swedish admiral ship the Vasa in 1628, just a few minutes after it was launched. At that time, the Swedish navy dominated the north seas, and this episode contributed to the decline in the power of the kingdom of Sweden. The museum was build around the ship after it was pulled up and restored around 1961.*

75 top *The Stockholm National Museum is the largest Swedish art collection in the world: it includes works from the sixteenth to the twentieth centuries, with 16,000 paintings and sculptures. There are also works by Swedish artists and artisans from the eighteenth to the twentieth centuries.*

75 center left *This statue of Gustav Vasa, the nation's founder, is on display at the Nordiska Museet. The museum, founded in 1907, shows Swedish life from 1520 to the present, with over a million and a half objects.*

75 center right *The Vasa was decorated with about 700 bas-relief sculptures, with subjects inspired by the Bible, the royal family, and classic mythology.*

75 bottom *Between 1620 and 1630, the Swedish Royal Navy, which up to then had dominated Baltic navigation routes, lost not only the Vasa, to which the well-known museum in Stockholm is dedicated, but also 14 more of its larger ships. With them went Sweden's dreams of power.*

76 top *The Skansen, the world's first open air museum, was opened in 1891 based on an idea by Artur Hazelius. Created to preserve vanishing memories of rural Sweden, the museum includes the architecture, objects, and atmospheres of bygone Sweden.*

76 bottom *The Skansen includes houses from every region in Sweden, with examples of different types of buildings: from mills to farms, warehouses to tanneries, and painter's studios to churches.*

76-77 *In one of Stockholm's city parks, frost and wind have traced shadows and seeming empty spaces that resemble complex embroidery.*

Beyond
the capital

78-79 *Drottningholm Castle is now the permanent residence of the royal family. It is on the UNESCO World Heritage List and has rococo and Gustavian interiors with French and Swedish furniture.*

79 top *Sailing through the Stockholm archipelago, we can see islands and reefs, canals and arms of the sea, villages and fortified towns. Ferries leaving from the city offer daily cruises, some with meals on board.*

79 bottom *Gripsholm Castle in Mariefred, built in the sixteenth century, reflects in the frozen surface of Lake Mälaren.*

Göteborg: The Merchant City

80-81 *Vessels from the East India Shipping Company once sailed from the port of Göteborg. Later, Swedish emigrants left for America from here. Now the port serves only tourists, many of whom arrive from Denmark and the Netherlands.*

81 top *The Stora Theater in Göteborg on Kungsportsavenyen, an airy boulevard better known as "Avenyen," was opened in 1859.*

81 center *Gustav II Adolf of Göteborg Square, with the former bourse, the old seventeenth century city hall, and the present-day one, is the city's administrative and political center.*

81 bottom *Splendid seventeenth and eighteenth century buildings face the "Grand Canal" of Göteborg. The city, which was razed to the ground by the Danes in the seventeenth century, was rebuilt according to a Dutch design.*

82-83 *The bell tower of the church of St. Christina (seventeenth century), with its 42 bell carillon, rises alongside the building that is the headquarters of the Swedish East India Shipping Company. The company dominated trade during the eighteenth and nineteenth centuries, with enormous profits that benefited the entire city.*

84-85 *Neptune's Fountain by Carl Milles (1931) adorns Götaplatsen in Göteborg. While the statue of the sea god has become a symbol of the city, the square, designed for the 1923 World's Fair, is the city's cultural center, with the Museum of Art, the Concert Hall, and the Hasselblad Center.*

85 top *The building that holds the old bourse, which dates back to 1849, is on Gustav II Adolf Square. The city was a leading financial center during the times of the East India Company, and continued to lead during industrialization, when companies like SKF and Volvo were founded.*

85 center *Over recent years, Göteborg has become a shopping hub, with entire streets bursting with shops offering merchandise at any price, from Avenyn to Kungsgatan to Fredsgatan. There are also many shopping centers, one of which is pictured in this photo.*

85 bottom *In Göteborg, the fish market is held in a building constructed in 1874. Open from Tuesday to Saturday, it offers the best of products from Sweden's western coast.*

86-87 *The equestrian statue of Charles X dominates Stortorget, the main square in Malmö. It faces City Hall, which dates back to the sixteenth century.*

Malmö: The Danish City

88-89 *Canals surround the historic district of Malmö, including the Danish fortress of Malmöhus, which now houses a museum. It is an especially interesting water network, as it also includes park areas.*

89 left *St. Peter's Church in Malmö was built in 1319. The exterior is red brick and reflects Baltic Gothic style. The interior has a soaring nave and aisles, and the transept has two naves.*

89 top right *Lilla Torget is the most Danish of the squares in Malmö. The fifteenth century lattice-work houses and cobblestone pavements create an extremely inviting atmosphere. This district of restaurants and outdoor cafes is lively until late at night.*

89 right center *The walls of the Merchants' Chapel in St. Peter's Church are adorned with late Gothic frescoes. The interior of the church also has a late sixteenth century pulpit that depicts episodes from the life of Jesus, and a magnificent seventeenth century retable.*

89 bottom right *Malmöhus fortress was built by the Danish king Christian III in the sixteenth century to control traffic in the Öresund, the strait that separates Malmö from Copenhagen, now traversed by a tunnel bridge.*

Uppsala: The Intellectual City

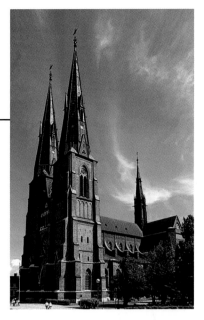

90 *This splendid window is from Uppsala Cathedral, built between 1270 and 1435. Rebuilt in 1705 after a fire, in the late nineteeth century two towers were added; at 387 feet high, they are as tall as the church is long. Erik the Saint, patron of Sweden, Gustav Vasa, and Carolus Linnaeus are buried here.*

91 top left *The beautiful Uppsala Cathedral represents almost all epochs: it was destroyed and rebuilt five times, and its styles and periods thus overlap. Suffice it to note the thirteenth century gate, the fifteenth century sculptures at the entry, the fourteenth century apse, and the eighteenth century pulpit.*

91 bottom left *In 1644, Queen Christina was crowned in the castle of Gustav Vasa, built in 1539 but reconstructed in the eighteenth century.*

91 top right *Fifth to ninth century Viking kings are buried around the church of Erik the Saint in Gamla Uppsala, the "Old City."*

91 center right *The Fyrisån traverses the city of Uppsala, running right through the historic center. Uppsala is home to many university students involved in scientific and technological research.*

91 bottom right *Bicycling along one of the bridges between Östra and Västragatan: a rather frequent sight in Uppsala, bicycles are the most popular mode of transportation in the historic center, especially with the many students who live in the city.*

92 top left *This narrow, winding street leads to Uppsala's Old City, which is now a little village two and a half miles from the downtown area. To the left, we can see one of the* Viking *tumuli that still hold so many secrets.*

92 bottom left *Hammarby, located southeast of Uppsala, was the summer residence of Carolus Linnaeus. This great scientist, who wrote Systema Naturae, taught some of his lessons at his country house, where he had a collection of Siberian plants.*

92 top right *The old church in Uppsala's Old City is a fine brick building that stands on the site of a former pagan temple.*

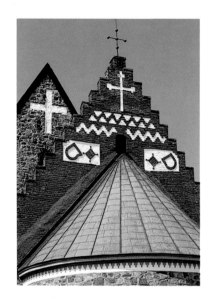

92 bottom right *The offices of the University of Uppsala, the oldest university in Scandinavia (1477), with the entry hall shown here, are in a palace rebuilt in the nineteenth century in Renaissance style. Visitors can see the Chancellery Room and the throne of Gustav Adolf (1631).*

92-93 *Gustav III, who ruled until the late eighteenth century, urged artists and artisans to develop a national style, the so-called Gustavian style. He accomplished this by embracing neoclassical ideas and encouraging a certain lightness of lines, which can be seen in this dwelling in Lövstabruk.*

Little Ones from the South

94 top left *Kalmar, with one of the roads in the old city shown here, is one of the oldest towns in Sweden. The Kalmar treaty was signed here in 1397, uniting the crowns of Denmark, Norway, and Sweden.*

94 center left *The city of Kalmar is on the Baltic Sea, protected by the long island of Öland. Its inland area is especially famous for artisan and industrial workshops devoted to glass-working.*

94 bottom left *Lilla Torget, Kalmar's "little square," is surrounded by the Bishop's and Governor's palaces. In old Swedish cities, there is always a large and a small square that hold the most important symbols of municipal power.*

94 right *Kalmar Castle, surrounded by inlets and massive walls with square turrets, is an example of a fortress from the era of Swedish domination in the Baltic area. One of the most interesting areas is Erik XIV's room, visible in the photograph.*

94-95 *In this view of Kalmar from above, we can see the hulking castle. Built in the thirteenth century and reconstructed in the fourteenth century, with seven covered towers, the castle is one of the best preserved in the country.*

Medieval Sites

96-97 *Every year in Visby, the little capital of Gotland, there is an extremely popular Medieval Week, with countless people in costume, events, tournaments, and games. The city gives the festival its atmosphere, ruins, and old walls.*

97 left *Like all the old churches on the island, St. Mary's, Visby's cathedral, has a Catholic past (and a Romanesque and Gothic style). With the Reformation, it was adapted to Protestantism's more sober forms.*

97 top right *St. Catherine's in Visby is the emblem of Catholic churches abandoned after the Reformation. The skeleton that remains emphasizes even more clearly the beautiful Gothic forms soaring toward the sky and the architectural lightness.*

97 bottom right *The medieval walls of Visby, 33 feet high with 38 towers running along two miles, are an imposing work that underscores Visby's importance during the period of high medieval Baltic trade.*

98 top left *The famous Ales Stenar near Ystad, in the village of Kåseberga, is an Iron Age tomb formed of 60 blocks of stone that trace a ship 42 feet long and 66 feet wide.*

98 center left *With its numerous lattice-work houses, the town of Ystad has a medieval design; its little harbor lies on the southern coast of Sweden. The region's relative seclusion detracts nothing from it, with its long, white sand beaches and somewhat more continental light.*

98 bottom left *The Gothic St. Peter's Church (fourteenth to fifteenth century) in Ystad, with the nearby fifteenth century Franciscan monastery, holds collections from the Local History Society.*

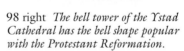

98 right *The bell tower of the Ystad Cathedral has the bell shape popular with the Protestant Reformation.*

98-99 *The historic center of the town of Ystad still has many historic buildings, especially from the seventeenth and eighteenth centuries. Emblematic is the old Pharmacy, a wooden structure from the seventeenth century, which holds a collection of antique vases.*

100 top left *The façade of the Lund Cathedral, in Romanesque style with German-Rhine influence, was remodeled over the course of the centuries, as was the rest of the edifice. It is framed by two imposing towers that city residents call "Lund's children."*

100 bottom left *This image of the interior of the Lund Cathedral, with a nave and two aisles, emphasizes the structure of the apse. Of particular interest is the crypt, which holds the tombs of archbishops from the twelfth century to the Reformation.*

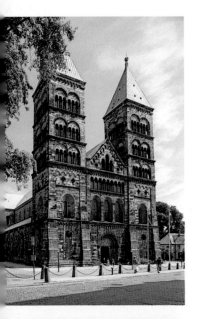

100 right *The Cathedral's fourteenth century astronomical clock, one of Lund's attractions, chimes every hour and at noon and 3 p.m. (at 1 p.m. and 3 p.m. on Sunday), setting in motion the Three Kings.*

100-101 *The Lund Cathedral is the oldest and most important church in Sweden. It originated in the edifice that Saint Knut, patron of Denmark, built in 1085. One of the Danish kings convinced the Pope that Scandinavia deserved a diocese, and so the north separated from Hamburg. No expense was spared in building the cathedral, dedicated to the Virgin Mary and Saint Lawrence.*

Nature's Dominion

102 top *Lapp boundaries are ambiguous: the only ones are those established by Scandinavian settlers. Lapp territory runs from the Kola Peninsula to the Norwegian Sea.*

102 bottom *In the winter, Lapp lakes, completely frozen up to Talvatis as shown in this photo, are the best transit routes for snowmobiles and an open field for reindeer-drawn sleds.*

103 *This church is located in the Lapp area of Jokkmokk. Before conversion to Christianity in the seventeenth century, the Sami practiced a religion based on ancestors and natural forces such as the thunder, wind, sun, and moon. The intermediary between man and nature was the shaman, known as the noaide.*

104-105 *Firs, Scotch pines, white birches, dwarf birches, and Lapland willows; blueberries and other berries, bladder-campion and ranunculus, potentilla and veronica, and many lichens: plant life in Lapland is as spare as its terrain.*

106-107 *The largest igloo in the world, the ice hotel, is located in the village of Jukkasjärvi in Lapland, a few miles from Kiruna. Inside temperatures are about 19°F.*

107 top *The ice hotel has about 30 rooms and a "honeymoon suite."*

107 bottom *The idea of an ice hotel comes naturally, although here traditional houses are made of hide or wood. The hotel has been extremely popular with tourists, who enjoy every comfort despite the truly unusual climate conditions.*

108-109 *The aurora borealis is one of the most disquieting yet fascinating natural phenomena in the world. The lights were once a source of terror, a curse by enemies, the spirits of the dead, bringers of misfortune.*

110-111 *The rivers that flow into the Gulf of Bothnia have their source in the mountains at the edge of Norway.*

112 top *The marshy areas of Lapland are the realm of billions of little mosquitoes that need the short summer season to complete their life cycle. They are thus especially fierce, and mushrooms and bark need to be burned to combat them.*

112 center *Summer fishing in Lapland uses traditional techniques. However, in the winter a portable drill is used to make holes in the ice, a short pole is inserted in the hole, and the fisherman waits confidently. The fish, who have little food available, promptly take the bait.*

112 bottom *The Abisko National Park in Lapland may be one of the most spectacular parks in the world. Visitors can see Arctic foxes, lemmings, wild reindeer, bears, ermine minks, lynxes, squirrels, and Arctic partridges. In addition to conifers, there are snow gentians, bladder-campions, dryas, and angelica.*

112-113 *Early autumn in the Abisko National Park is tinged with the colors of the birches whose brilliant green summer leaves turn gold, while a first sprinkling of snow crowns the mountains in the background. The Abiskojokk River runs placidly among the vegetation.*

114 *Cotton-grass flowers on the shores of a little mountain lake. Once again Lapland offers an idyllic, utterly peaceful picture. The mountains, which in general are rather low (maximum altitude, 6926 feet and rounded, act as a watershed for Norway, making this part of Sweden a gentle slope down to the Golf of Bothnia.*

115 *Abiskojokk Canyon, about a mile long, was carved by water to a depth of 66 feet. It is one of the marvels of Abisko Park, whose name in Sami means "ocean forest," given its proximity to the Atlantic and the oceanic influence on local climate.*

116-117 *Sarek, the most remote of the parks, expresses the essence of wild nature due to deep valleys, great plateaus, sharp peaks, and broad glaciers. The Rapa River creates a wide valley, with great forests of birch and willow and colorful mountain flora.*

118-119 *Golden birches, green firs, a stormy sky, and stepped waterfalls create a fascinating natural picture. This is the essence of Lapland: orderly nature still bursting with power.*

119 top *The* lavvu, *a Lapp traveling tent, is easy to set up by interweaving long poles and covering them with hides and cloth.*

119 bottom *The great Lake Torneträsk, 43 miles long, winds through Abisko and along the Norwegian border. The railway built to carry iron from Kiruna to the port of Narvik in Norway also runs along the lake valley.*

120-121 *Young reindeer are marked in June and July by cutting the lower part of the animal's ear. To the Sami, reindeer are part of their identity and culture, as well as an irreplaceable means of subsistence.*

Lapp Life

122 top and center *The campfire is used to cook fish, soften dried meat, and prepare large pots of coffee.*

122 bottom *Castrated animals are used to pull transport sleds, which now carry tourists as well.*

122-123 *A timeless, universal image: man and his fire remind us that humans are bound to their source of survival.*

124 *This Sami face is framed with typical Lapp elements, like the fur-edged jacket and hood; but that veil of lace that appears on the forehead belies Swedish influence. The Uralian features of the face are still quite evident.*

125 left *The Lap market in Jokkmokk in February is the oldest in the region , dating back to 1605 (it is held from the first Wednesday to the first Saturday in February). Since the 1950's, it has seen a rebirth due to tourism, with more than 500 sales booths, a reindeer race, tasting of local dishes, and shows, music, and dances. It is a real party.*

125 top right *There are also religious ceremonies during market days in Jokkmokk: baptisms, weddings, and funerals are traditionally celebrated in the local eighteenth century church.*

125 bottom right *During market days in Jokkmokk, you can find almost anything, from Lap knives to dried reindeer meat. There are interesting hides and gray canvas cloth, traditional clothing, jackets, gloves, shoes, and fishing gear. The market allows visitors to come into contact with a culture hovering between tradition and modernity, with an equal love for reindeer and snowmobiles.*

126 top *Reindeer races are a strong tradition among the Lapps, despite the fact that reindeer are essentially indolent animals who are not really made for this kind of activity: accustomed to fleeing, reindeer move in disorganized fashion to disorient pursuers and are only capable of short bursts of speed. So the race is really a gamble, as it is difficult to guess what the animal will actually do.*

126 bottom *Over just a few years, traditional animal-drawn sleds have been joined and often replaced by snowmobiles, which have become indispensable for both winter travel and working with reindeer. Those who*

use these vehicles, such as the man shown here, clearly enjoy their practicality. Snowmobiles have become a new accessory or dependence, an object of worship like automobiles are in the West.

126-127 *Wearing skis, reindeer-race competitors use a rope to tie themselves to the animal's harness, then allow themselves to be dragged to the finish line. These races have the air of a folk festival.*

128 *A small procession of reindeer crossing the road as they look after their young is an emblematic image of one of Sweden's possible syntheses: reindeer and Volvos, respective symbols of pristine nature and avant-garde technology.*

Photo Credits:

Marcello Bertinetti/Archivio White Star: pages 122 top left, 122 center, 122-123.

Angelo Colombo/Archivio White Star: Map pages 8-9.

Giulio Veggi/Archivio White Star: pages. 1, 16 top, 17 top, 17 bottom, 18-19, 23 top, 26, 26-27, 30-31, 34 top, 36 center, 36 bottom, 36-37, 41 center, 41 bottom, 42-43, 43 top, 43 bottom, 50 top, 50 bottom, 50-51, 52-53, 53, 60, 61, 62 top right, 62 bottom left, 62 top right, 62 bottom left, 62 top right, 62-63, 66 top 67, 68, 69 top, 69 bottom, 72-73, 73 bottom right, 75 center right, 76 top right, 76 bottom left, 78-79, 79 top, 81top right, 81 center right, 82-83, 84-85, 85 center right, 85 bottom right, 86-87, 89 center right, 89 bottom right, 89 left, 90, 91 top left, 91 top right, 92 top left, 92 top right, 94 center left, 94 bottom left, 97 top left, 97 top right, 97 bottom right, 98 center left, 98 bottom left, 98 top right, 98-99, 100 top left, 100 bottom left, 100 top right, 100-101, 102 top, 102 bottom, 103, 104-105, 106-107, 107 top right, 107 bottom right, 110-111, 112 top left, 112 center left, 112 bottom left, 119 top right, 119 bottom right, 122 bottom, 124, 125 left, 125 top right, 125 bottom right, 128.

Stefano Amantini/Atlantide: pages 36 top, 41 top, 50 center, 58-59.

Andrea Battaglini: page 23 bottom.

Massimo Borchi/Atlantide: pages 22, 76-77, 126 bottom.

Lars Dahlstrom/Tiofoto: pages 32-33.

Nevio Doz: pages 72 top left, 72 bottom left, 74-75.

Peter Dyballa/Myra Naturfoto: pages 12-13

Ove Eriksson/Tiofoto: pages 38-39, 64-65.

Tomas Franklin/Myra Bildarkiv AB: pages 7, 16 bottom, 38, 48-49.

Sten Gustafsson/Myra Bildarkiv AB: page 28 top.

Leif Gustavsson/Myra Bildarkiv AB: pages 14-15, 94-95

Tore Hagmann/Bruce Coleman Collection: pages 56-57, 118-119

Anders Jarnmark/Myra Bildarkiv AB: pages 46-47.

Birger Lallo/Myra Bildarkiv AB: pages 40-41, 54-55.

Roine Magnusson/Bruce Coleman Collection: page 24 top.

Susy Mezzanotte: pages 28-29, 66 top, 75 top right, 98 top left.

Nils-Johan Norenlind/Tiofoto: pages 88-89, 89 top right.

Flavio Pagani: pages 2-3, 28 bottom, 70-71, 79 bottom right, 81 bottom right, 85 top right, 91 bottom left, 91 center right, 91 bottom right, 92 bottom right, 92-93, 94 top left, 94 top right.

Jan Rietz/Tiofoto: pages 56 top, 96-97.

Giovanni Rinaldi/Il Dagherrotipo page 34 bottom.

Torbjon Skogedal/Myra Bildarkiv AB: pages 4-5, 44-45, 80-81.

Bjorn Svensson/Myra Bildarkiv AB: pages 24 bottom, 49, 56 bottom, 116-117.

Ph. S. Tauqueur/Franca Speranza: pages 24-25.

Valerio Travi: pages 20-21, 75 bottom right, 75 bottom left, 92 bottom right, 126 top, 126-127.

Thomas Utsi: pages 10-11, 108-109, 112-113, 114, 115, 120-121.

World Pict./Simephoto: page 6.

Hans Wretling/Tiofoto: page 35.